LUPITA NYONG'O

GROUNDBREAKING ACTOR

by Rachel Rose

Minneapolis, Minnesota

Credits

Cover and title page, © Roy Rochlin/Getty Images; 4, © Araya Doheny/Stringer/Getty Images; 5, © Jaguar PS/Shutterstock; 6, © Featureflash Photo Agency/Shutterstock; 7, © Robin Marchant/Stringer/Getty Images; 8, © Sven Manguard Wikimedia; 10, © Vivien Killilea/Contributor/Getty Images; 11, © George Pimentel/Contributor/Getty Images; 12, © Walter McBride/Contributor/Getty Images; 13, © Johnny Nunez/Contributor/Getty Images; 14, © Faiz Zaki/Shutterstock; 15, © Jeff Vespa/VF14/Contributor/Getty Images; 16, © Michael Kovac/Contributor/Getty Images; 17, © Raymond Hall/Contributor/Getty Images; 18, © Chelsea Guglielmino/Staff/Getty Images; 19, © Frederick M. Brown/Stringer/Getty Images; 20, © Freckle Films/CAA Media Finance/Album/Newscom; 21, © Future Publishing/Contributor/Getty Images

Bearport Publishing Company Product Development Team

President: Jen Jenson; Director of Product Development: Spencer Brinker; Senior Editor: Allison Juda; Editor: Charly Haley; Associate Editor: Naomi Reich; Senior Designer: Colin O'Dea; Associate Designer: Elena Klinkner; Associate Designer: Kayla Eggert; Product Development Assistant: Anita Stasson

Library of Congress Cataloging-in-Publication Data

Names: Rose, Rachel, 1968- author.
Title: Lupita Nyong'o : groundbreaking actor / by Rachel Rose.
Description: Minneapolis, Minnesota : Bearport Publishing Company, [2023] |
Series: Bearport biographies | Includes bibliographical references.
Identifiers: LCCN 2022033667 (print) | LCCN 2022033668 (ebook) | ISBN
9798885094030 (library binding) | ISBN 9798885095259 (paperback) | ISBN
9798885096409 (ebook)
Subjects: LCSH: Nyong'o, Lupita--Juvenile literature. | Motion picture
actors and actresses--Kenya--Biography--Juvenile literature. |
Actresses, Black--Kenya--Biography--Juvenile literature.
Classification: LCC PN2991.8.N96 R67 2023 (print) | LCC PN2991.8.N96
(ebook) | DDC 791.4302/8092 [B]--dc23/eng/20220914
LC record available at https://lccn.loc.gov/2022033667
LC ebook record available at https://lccn.loc.gov/2022033668

Copyright © 2023 Bearport Publishing Company. All rights reserved. No part of this publication may be reproduced in whole or in part, stored in any retrieval system, or transmitted in any form or by any means, electronic, mechanical, photocopying, recording, or otherwise, without written permission from the publisher.

For more information, write to Bearport Publishing, 5357 Penn Avenue South, Minneapolis, MN 55419.

Contents

A Young Winner 4

An Early Start 6

Finding Fame 10

Pursuing Passions 16

What's Next? 20

Timeline 22

Glossary 23

Index 24

Read More 24

Learn More Online 24

About the Author 24

A Young Winner

Lupita Nyong'o cried tears of joy as she held her **award**. The crowd clapped and cheered for the young actor who just won the 2014 Oscar for Best Supporting Actress. It was Lupita's first role in a major movie, and she had just earned one of the biggest awards in the business.

Lupita's first movie, *12 Years a Slave*, was a hit! She won many awards for her part in it.

Lupita was 29 when she got the part.

Lupita with her Oscar

An Early Start

Lupita was born on March 1, 1983, in Mexico City, Mexico. Soon, her family moved to Kenya, where her parents were from. As a child, Lupita's parents always **encouraged** her to follow her dreams. Her family often watched plays together, and Lupita knew she loved acting from a young age.

Lupita is the second oldest of six children. She is very close with her younger brother, Peter.

Lupita and Peter (right)

Lupita's mother, Dorothy *(left)*, continues to support her daughter.

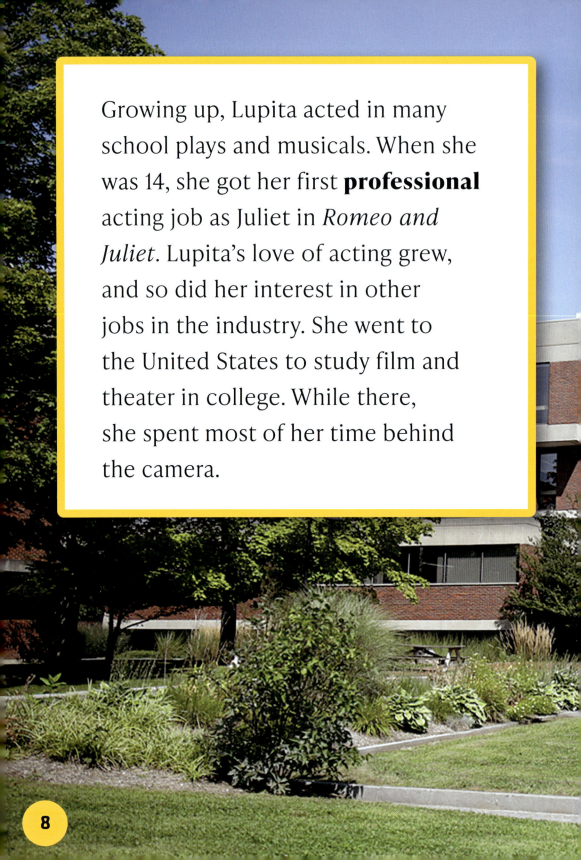

Growing up, Lupita acted in many school plays and musicals. When she was 14, she got her first **professional** acting job as Juliet in *Romeo and Juliet*. Lupita's love of acting grew, and so did her interest in other jobs in the industry. She went to the United States to study film and theater in college. While there, she spent most of her time behind the camera.

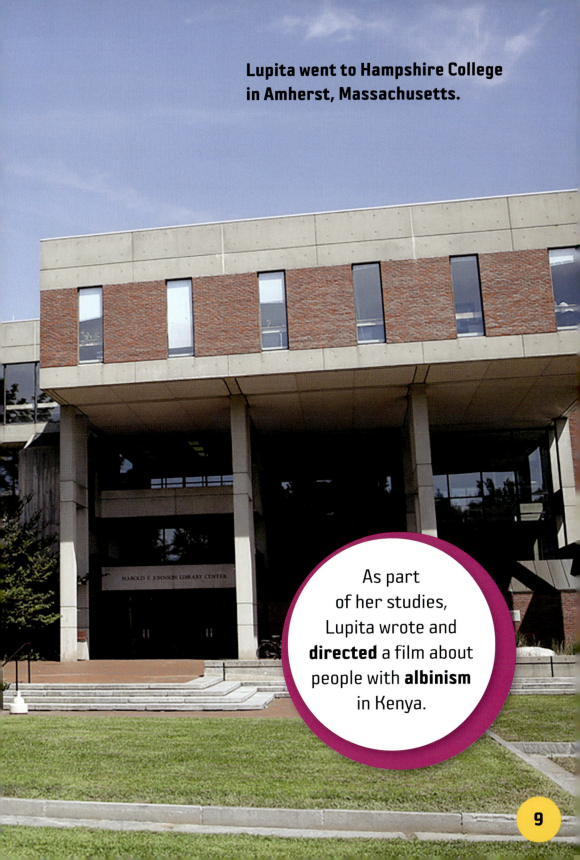

Lupita went to Hampshire College in Amherst, Massachusetts.

As part of her studies, Lupita wrote and **directed** a film about people with **albinism** in Kenya.

Finding Fame

Then, Lupita decided to follow her childhood dream to be in front of the camera. She got a few parts in smaller films and television shows. In 2010, she went back to school for acting. Before she even graduated, Lupita got her big break. She earned a major part in the movie *12 Years a Slave*.

Lupita *(second from the left)* with the director and other actors from the film

Lupita and director Steve McQueen *(right)*

The director of *12 Years a Slave* saw more than 1,000 actors for Lupita's part before he gave her the job!

Lupita quickly became famous for her talent. Soon, she was able to choose roles that were important to her. She wanted to show the stories of people that are not often seen in movies and plays. In 2016, Lupita was in her first **Broadway** play. It was called *Eclipsed*. The show was the first one on Broadway to have a cast and crew of all Black women.

The poster for *Eclipsed* above a theater on Broadway

Lupita and her costars take a bow at the end of the show.

Lupita hoped *Eclipsed* would encourage other people to share their stories.

Both on the screen and on the stage, Lupita played many characters. She loved the **challenge** of taking on different parts. Lupita was a space **pirate** in several *Star Wars* movies. She also voiced characters in a few **animated** films. And in 2018, she began her role in the movie series *Black Panther*.

Lupita was excited for Black children to see a superhero that looked like them when they watched *Black Panther*.

Lupita with *Black Panther* star Chadwick Boseman *(left)*

Pursuing Passions

Acting is not Lupita's only **passion**. She wants to be a role model, too. As a kid, Lupita was teased because her skin was darker than that of her brothers and sisters. She didn't look like people in popular movies. Now, she uses her success to show kids that they are beautiful as they are.

Lupita speaks about all the things that can make people beautiful.

Lupita wrote a book based on the challenges she faced growing up. It's about learning how to love yourself.

Lupita cares about women's rights, too. When she was young, her father taught her the importance of **equality**. He told her women can do anything. Lupita shares that same lesson and often gives speeches in support of women's rights. She is also part of several **organizations** that help women around the world.

In 2018, Lupita spoke in front of thousands of people at the Women's March on Washington. The event was for women's equality.

Lupita also ecourages other actors to support women.

What's Next?

Lupita worked hard to make her childhood dreams come true. She has acted in movies and plays. She is a role model and encourages people to follow their dreams. Lupita plans to keep acting and use her success to fight for girls and women everywhere. Lupita has more she wants to do—and she will work hard to get it done!

In her 2022 movie *The 355*, Lupita played an international spy alongside an all-star female cast.

Timeline

Here are some key dates in Lupita Nyong'o's life.

1983
Born on March 1

1997
Lands her first acting job

2007
Graduates from college

2014
Wins an Oscar for her role in *12 Years a Slave*

2015
Plays a space pirate in *Star Wars*

2016
Gets her first role on Broadway

2019
Publishes a book for children

2022
Returns to her role in *Black Panther: Wakanda Forever*

22

Glossary

albinism a condition that makes skin, hair, and eyes very pale or white

animated produced by the creation of a series of drawings or pictures that appear to move

award a prize for being the best at something

Broadway a famous area in New York City with many large theaters

challenge a difficult problem or task that requires extra effort

directed told actors what to do in a movie or play

encouraged supported another person

equality the right for everyone to be treated the same way

organizations groups of people with common interests or purposes

passion something one cares about very deeply

pirate a person who attacks and steals from ships

professional done by people who are paid

Index

Black Panther 14-15, 22
Broadway 12, 22
college 8-9, 22
Eclipsed 12-13
Kenya 6, 9
Oscar 4-5, 22
rights 18
role model 16, 20
Star Wars 14, 22
theater 8, 12
12 Years a Slave 4, 10-11, 22

Read More

Keppeler, Jill. *Be an Activist! (Be the Change! Shaping Your Community)*. New York: Gareth Stevens Publishing, 2019.

Watson, Stephanie. *Lupita Nyong'o (Influential People)*. North Mankato, MN: Capstone Press, 2020.

Learn More Online

1. Go to **www.factsurfer.com** or scan the QR code below.
2. Enter "**Lupita Nyong'o**" into the search box.
3. Click on the cover of this book to see a list of websites.

About the Author

Rachel Rose is a writer who lives in San Francisco. Her favorite books to write are about people who lead inspiring lives.

24